BERMUDA
Aerial Views
SCOTT STALLARD

AUGUST '93

OAKWELL

BOULTON

THIS BOOK IS DEDICATED TO
MARGARET AND SIDNEY STALLARD

Photographs © Scott Stallard, Bermuda
Designed by Sheena McKenzie, Toronto
Produced by Boulton, Howard & King, Assocs., Toronto
ISBN 0-920831-12-9

Printed and bound in Hong Kong by Book Art Inc., Toronto

ACKNOWLEDGEMENTS

As with all long-term projects, there are those to whom thanks are due for their contributions towards the final result. The first is Sharon Forrest, for her editing skills on the word-processor and her support throughout the year. Then there is my photographic assistant in the helicopter, Sabine Berg, who kept me in film and on course throughout the shooting. Leslie Todd parted with a generous supply of advice and information, gained the year before on a helicopter shoot, and Wendell Hollis helped in the captioning with his knowledge of Bermuda homes and properties. Eddie Marshall of Bermuda Photocraftsmen and his refreshingly efficient staff processed my film faster than I could review it! Over two hundred rolls came back to my complete satisfaction. Finally, a 'thank you' to those friends whose encouragement and loyalty have not gone unnoticed, Mike Spurling, Robert and Gail Henderson, Robert Stigwood, Teddy and Edna Tucker, Bill Reyman at K & L, my agent The Image Bank in New York City, and to Sheena McKenzie and Roger Boulton for bringing it all together.

SCOTT STALLARD
St George, Bermuda

INTRODUCTION

I was a year old when my father first flew over Bermuda photographing a landscape far different from that of today. Some thirty years later I was shown his slides and they set me on a course resulting in this book.

Knowing the interest Bermudians and visitors have in the island, I tried in vain to get up in every helicopter that came to Bermuda. In frustration I even researched the possibility of using a hot-air balloon, complete with advertising space on it. It would take me two years, but patience prevailed and shooting began from the open door of a helicopter in the summer of 1991.

Armed with three motor-driven Nikons fully loaded with Fujichrome Velvia, it was possible to record stills virtually every second, producing a collection of over six thousand colour transparencies. The images do not tell a story so much as beckon one to look into them, to search out the details or at least first discover the location, on an island we thought we knew so well.

It was windy, it was noisy, it was exhilarating! To see such beauty everywhere was simply euphoric. With so much to photograph I knew immediately I would need another hundred rolls of film. The excitement continued on into the evening after picking up the processed slides. It was like discovering treasure when I came across great shots on the light-box, viewing vast areas from one vantage point, and satisfying my curiosity by seeing for the first time so many properties previously hidden behind tall hedges and dry stone walls.

Back up the next morning to continue the project,

spotting a derelict cottage, weathered grey and overgrown, committed to memory in order to be reshot the next time around. Heading up South Shore, keeping the sun behind us, changing lenses and marvelling at the beaches beyond compare. It strikes me that from this height everything is blue, white and green.

Rounding Wreck Hill we fly over Elys Harbour, recording the peace and tranquillity hundreds of feet below, perhaps my favourite spot west of St George! Dockyard comes up quickly on our left with the *Queen Elizabeth II* having berthed earlier alongside, as evidenced by the silt she has stirred up. A fishing boat towing dinghies laden with nets sits off Boaz Island, inviting at least a half a roll of film be spent. Back down through Southampton past Five Star Island, thinking how fortunate so many people are to have an ocean view. Magnificent homes appearing one after another, so few small cottages to be seen. A preponderance of pools for an island where the ocean is clean, warm and within minutes of every home. Golf courses graphically set against the pink sands and aquamarine waters; shipwrecks visible from our unique vantage point, and meticulously manicured gardens, lawns and hedges. The scene resembles a model until the people start waving.

At 500 feet over the city of Hamilton, you can see the hustle and bustle below; you know what it sounds like, but you cannot hear it. The deep sound of the engine rotors and static on the microphone are so incongruous with the view, perhaps a little calypso instead!

Continuing the shoot eastward we cross Harrington Sound, sighting snorkelers between Cockroach Island and Abbotts Cliff, passing Trinity Church nestled in the bay further along, and up over the hill, turning slightly, as my attention focuses on the unique layout of the Perfume Factory gardens. Although they border the main road and I drive by them every day, suddenly it is all new to me. This is undoubtedly the greatest thrill of seeing Bermuda from the air. What has been viewed all our lives from one perspective is magically transformed to another, where you must look two or three times at your own home and its surroundings because you don't immediately recognize it. To experience this is to discover a new Bermuda. It is a discovery that this chain of islands is even more beautiful than we knew it to be. There are no disappointments up here, even the roundabouts with their floral designs become photogenic. The overwhelming impression is that the people of Bermuda take great pride in their homes and their environment. When this is combined with that which nature has provided, the poincianas in bloom, red and white oleander, pink and white beaches sandwiched between weathered coral and clean clear water, blue-green and all the colours in between, we see the images that follow.

SCOTT STALLARD
St George

1 Bermuda from the east

4 Looking southeast across the City of
   Hamilton and its harbour

5 Nellie's Walk and the City Hall fountain
   pool, Church Street, Hamilton

6 'Huntley Tower' and northern views across
   Hamilton Harbour

7 The cruise ship *Westward* alongside
   Dockyard at the western end of the Island

10 The gardens of the Bermuda Perfumery

11 Traditional Bermuda roofstyle,
    Mid-Ocean Club, Tucker's Town

12 The 14th Green, Riddell's Bay Golf Course, Warwick

13 'Granaway', Harbour Road, Warwick

14 'Somerville', Middle Road, Smiths

15 The 'Map of Bermuda' pond, Gibbon's Gardens, Devonshire

16 'Windsong', Riddell's Bay, Warwick

17 The point at 'Willowbank',
    Elys Harbour, Sandys

18 The ferry approaching Two Rock Passage, the entrance to Hamilton Harbour

19 The St George Club time-share cottages, overlooking St George Harbour and golf course

20 'Grey Gables', Riddell's Bay, Warwick

21 Yacht at Hinson's Island, stocking up for its voyage north

24 The old beach pavilion, 'Southlands',
South Shore, Warwick

25 Working the fields, 'Locust Hall',
Devonshire

26 'Simon's Cottage', High Point,
Southampton

27 'Donaghmore', Tucker's Town

28 'Overlook', overlooking Hamilton Harbour

29 'Five Star Island', Southampton

30 'Flying Colours', Cavello Bay, Sandys

31 'Palmetto House', a National Trust property, North Shore, Devonshire

32 'Locust Hall', Middle Road, Devonshire

33 A fisherman with bait-nets lies off Boaz Island, Sandys

34 Approaching Bermuda from the east

35 'Windyfields', South Shore, Southampton

36 'Mount Pleasant', Paget

37 'Crestwood', Paget

38 'Perot's Island', Riddell's Bay, Warwick

39 Fitted dinghies round the stake boat, Sunday races

40 'Celtic Green' overlooking Mid-Ocean Golf Course, Glebe Hill

41 'Coral Sea', South Shore, Smiths

44 Trinity Church, Baileys Bay

45 Clifftop homes along Harrington Sound, Smiths

46 Immaculate gardens of an island home

47 Hidden cottage and arable land

50 'Woodside', Middle Road, Devonshire

51 Northern view of Mangrove Bay and Cambridge Beaches

52 'Simon's Cottage', South Shore Cliffs, Southampton

53 'The Gables', Harbour Road, Paget

54 Eastern islands of St George Harbour

55 'Beach Cove', South Shore, Smiths

56 Riddell's Bay homes

57 'The Boathouse', Harrington Sound Road, Smiths

58 Christ Church and the old Devonshire
Church

59 The perfect getaway, Lantana Colony
Club, Somerset

60 Fitted dinghies at the stake boat await starter's orders

61 The Civil Air Terminal and U.S. naval base

62 'Mayflower' sits majestically amidst green space and arable land

63 Riddell's Bay homes and Golf Course, Warwick

66 'Valley Green' and 'Lizard's Leap', Granaway Deep, Warwick

67 Aberfeldy Nursery and views to the west

68 Government House and North Shore, Pembroke

69 The old railway pylons, Franks Bay, Southampton

70 Middle Road and Tee Street, Devonshire, looking west to the City of Hamilton

71 The stone quarry overlooking Harrington Sound, Smiths

72 'Burnt House', Granaway Deep, Warwick

73 Looking south over homes of Knapton Estates, Knapton Hill, Smiths

74 'Sunnylands', set amongst lush vegetation off Middle Road, Devonshire

75 The 18th tee, Mid-Ocean Golf Course, Tucker's Town

76 Views from Jenning's Land, over Flatts Inlet with Harrington Sound to the right

77 The Bermuda Aquarium Museum and Zoo, Flatts, Hamilton Parish

78 The Botanical Gardens, Paget

79 Marshland, opposite the Botanical
Gardens, South Shore

80 Looking east from Southampton Princess,
down the South Shore beaches

81 Horseshoe Beach, Southampton

82 Tucker's Town houses, from Castle
Harbour to South Shore

83 Long Island and the Boer War Cemetery
looking southeast across islands of the
Great Sound

84 Shell and Esso storage facilities at Ferry Reach, St George

85 Fitted dinghies on their first downwind run, spinnakers out, St George Harbour

86 'Flying Colours', Cavello Bay, Sandys

87 'Old Chimneys', Rocky Bay, Devonshire

88 Looking north over Castle Point, Castle Harbour

89 'Jungle' and 'Pink Chimneys', Castle Harbour, Tucker's Town

90 'Palm Grove', Gibbon's Gardens, Devonshire

91 'The Pampas', shoreline, South Shore, Smiths

92 Farmland and water catchments overlook Harrington Sound

93 'Fleetwood Manor' and 'Point House', Granaway Deep, Warwick

94 Fort Hamilton, overlooking East Broadway and Hamilton Harbour

95 Warwick Long Bay and South Shore Road

96 'Ercildoune', Point Shares, Pembroke

97 North shore road, Devonshire

100 Darrell's Marine Slip, Mills Creek, Pembroke

101 The Catholic Church graveyard, Roberts Avenue, Devonshire

102   St David's Cricket Club, 'Lords', and
      Cashew City, St David's Island

103   'Mangrove View', Devonshire with
      Camden and the Botanical Gardens
      to the northwest

104 Cruise ships along Front Street, City of Hamilton

105 Gibbs Hill Lighthouse atop Lighthouse Hill, Southampton

106 Rock formations, South Shore beaches, Warwick

107 'Lockward House', Harbour Road, Paget

108 St George Golf Course, Wellington Oval
and Ferry Reach

109 Abbotts Cliff, Harrington Sound,
Hamilton Parish

110 Horse trails along South Shore, Warwick

111 'The Clearing' Tucker's Town

112 Fern Island, property of the Fern Island Club

113 Fort St Catherine, landing site of Bermuda's first shipwrecked inhabitants

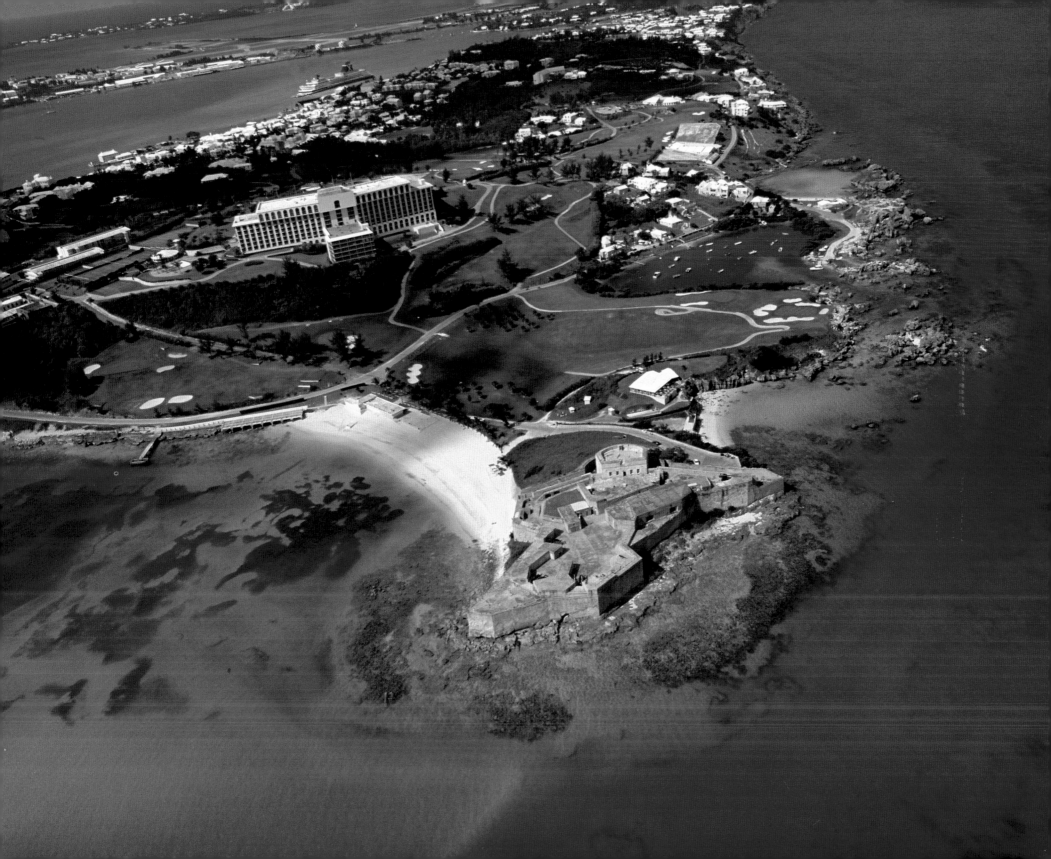

114 Looking southeast along Flatts Inlet, Hamilton Parish

115 Imported goods line the Hamilton Docks

118 Hillside homes, Point Shares, Pembroke

119 St John's Church and Sunday school,
Pembroke

120 'Banana' and 'Banana Cottage', Harrington Sound

121 Frick's Point, Tucker's Town

124   The surf rolls up onto Warwick Long Bay

125   'The Reefs', South Shore, Southampton

128 Jobson's Cove and horses on the trail, South Shore, Warwick

129 Hotel by the beach, South Shore, Warwick

130 'Cedarhurst', Wilkinson Avenue, Hamilton Parish

131 St George Golf Course meets North Shore

132 Lone windsurfer off the Western end of Somerset

133 'Cymru' along Castle Harbour, Tucker's Town

134 Protected cove, North Shore, Hamilton
Parish

135 'Durham', Old Slip Lane, overlooking
Hamilton Harbour

136 Abandoned cottage near Cobbs Hill, Warwick

137 Looking west along Harbour Road, Warwick

140 Boiler reefs, South Shore

141 Plants for sale, Aberfeldy Nursery, Paget

142 Fitted dinghies, 'Elizabeth', 'Challenger', 'Victory', 'Bloodhound', 'Contest' and 'Echo'

143 'Winton', North Shore, Devonshire

144 The beach at 'Blue Flag', Mangrove Bay, Somerset

145 Yacht tied off home on Hinson's Island, Hamilton Harbour

150 Snorklers between Cockroach Island and Abbots Cliff

151 'The Pampas' property, South Shore, Devonshire

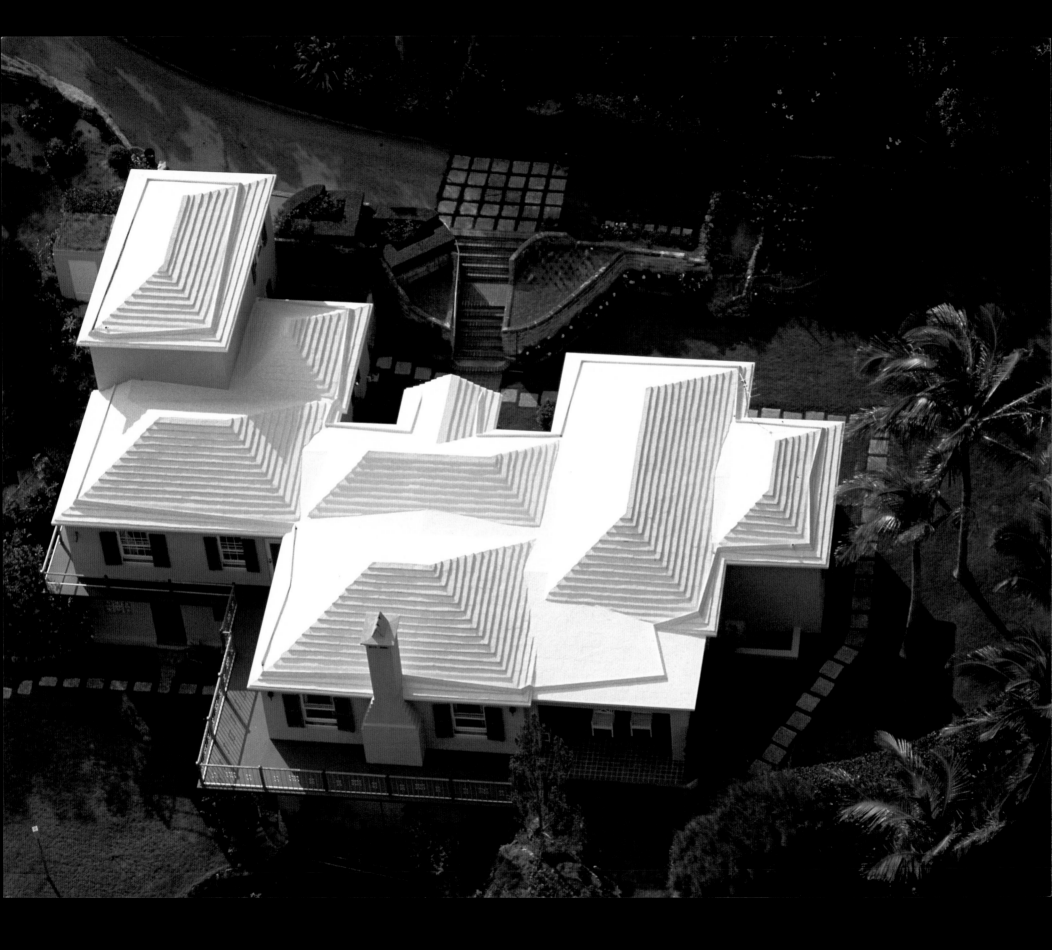

152 Bermuda slate roof, Tucker's Town Bay

153 Quarried stone along the waterside, Sandys

156 'Round House' and its lagoon, Tucker's Town

157 The causeway and area dredged to build the U.S. Base and Civil Air Terminal

158 Castle Island and Charles Island, Castle Harbour

159 Bathers frolic in the surf of Horseshoe Bay

160 The ferry passes Point Shares on its way to Dockyard

161 'Blue Flag', Mangrove Bay, Somerset

164 Little abandoned cottage, Grace Island

165 Remains of a wrecked boat, Elys
     Harbour, Sandys

166 Island home, Hamilton Harbour

167 The old town of St George

172 Cricket match in progress, Wellington Oval, St George

173 Arable land, looking north to St James Church, Sandys

174 'Blackwatch Pass' and southern views toward the City of Hamilton

175 Old wrecks lie in a bay along St George Harbour

176 A family watches the dinghy races from their roof, St George Harbour

177 Grey's Bridge, Sandys Parish

178 Homes along the beautiful Tucker's Town peninsula

179 Ordnance Island and the Town of St George

182 The *Queen Elizabeth II* alongside
     Dockyard, Sandys Parish

183 King's Castle, Castle Island, Castle
     Harbour

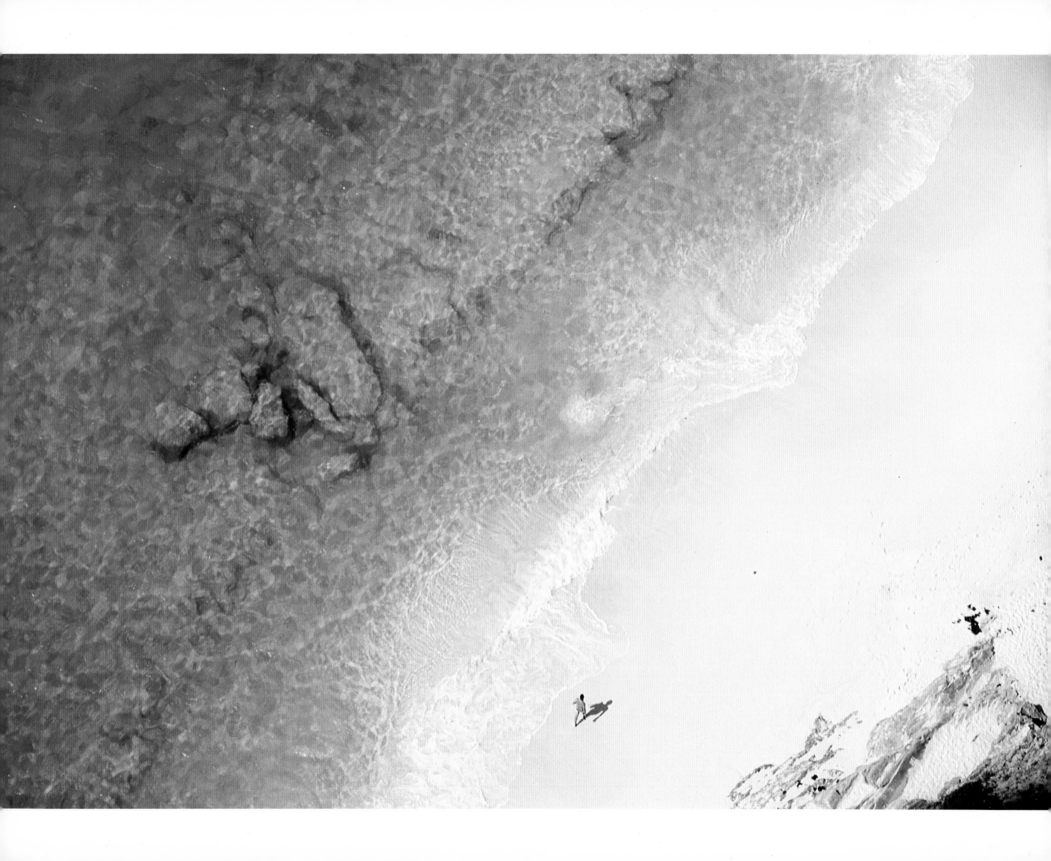

184 Walking the beach, South Shore, Warwick

185 Author in the helicopter

ABOUT THE AUTHOR

SCOTT STALLARD was born and raised in Bermuda. He attended school in Bermuda, England and the United States, graduating with a Bachelor of Science degree from Springfield College. Since then he has worked in the hotel and airline industry, as an actor and professional model in New York City, as an assistant to a film producer and is now a health club owner, but without doubt his prime interest has been photography.

A self-taught photographer, Scott is represented in New York by Image Bank, the world's largest stockphoto agency. His award-winning work has been featured on numerous magazine covers and widely exhibited.

Scott's first private showing of 42 original works, held at the Bermuda Aquarium and hosted by film producer Robert Stigwood, sold out in a few hours. He went on to produce over four hundred other prints for collectors of photographic art.

Scott's first two photographic books *Bermuda* and *Bermuda II* have sold over 10,000 copies, helping him to be nominated one of Two Outstanding Young People of 1990. Scott's fourth book, already in development, will feature his best work to date, including images from his 1991 trip to Nepal and China and of the hilltribes of Northern Thailand.

Scott is a member of the National Geographic Society, the Bermuda National Trust, the Bermuda Biological Station, the Bermuda Aquarium Museum and Zoo, the Bluebird Society, the St George Historical Society and the Bermuda Heritage Advisory Committee.